Friendship Bracel
Beyond The Basi

GW00383290

Friendship bracelets aren't just for kids anymore! These 19 designs show how easy it is to go beyond the basics of those knotted bracelet styles you love. Each one sparkles with beads, charms, or special techniques.

LEISURE ARTS, INC. • Maumelle, Arkansas

pink crystal beads

SHOPPING LIST

- ☐ pink embroidery floss
- ☐ 6 pink crystal bicone beads
- ☐ sewing needle that will fit through the beads

To make the Bracelet:

1. Cut five 36" floss lengths. Holding all floss lengths together, tie an overhand knot (page 31) about 2" from one end. Tape the knot down *(Fig. 1)*. The middle strand is the core strand that the knots are tied around. Thread the needle on the core strand.

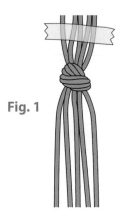

Fig. 1

2. Using 2 floss strands held together like a single strand, tie a square knot (page 31) around the core strand. Continue making square knots until you have 9 knots.

3. Slide a bead onto the core strand and tie 3 square knots *(Fig. 2)*. Continue adding beads and tying 3 square knots between beads until you add the last bead; tie 9 square knots.

Fig. 2

4. Holding all strands together, tie an overhand knot and trim the strands about 2" from the knot.

purple Disco ball beads

To make the Bracelet:

1. Hook the two clasp pieces together. Measure your wrist and decide how loose or tight you want your bracelet; subtract the clasp length. Divide this measurement by two.

2. Cut five 48" floss lengths. Cut two 12" floss lengths; set aside. Holding all five 48" lengths together, tape down the center of the strands *(Fig. 1)*. The middle strand is the core strand that the knots are tied around. Thread the needle on the core strand.

3. Referring to **Fig. 2**, slide a disco ball bead to the center of the core strand (next to the tape). Using 2 floss strands held together like a single strand, tie 2 square knots (page 31).

4. Slide a faceted bead onto the core strand and tie 2 square knots. Tying 2 square knots between beads, add 1 more disco ball and 1 more faceted bead. Tie square knots until the bracelet equals the measurement determined in Step 1.

5. Trim the strands to 2" and finish the ends (page 32) using the toggle clasp.

6. For the other side of the bracelet, remove the center tape piece and tie 2 square knots close to the center disco ball bead then repeat Steps 4-5.

Fig. 1

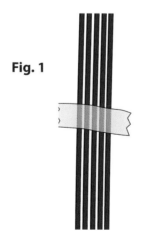

Fig. 2

aqua charms

To make the Bracelet:

1. Hook the two clasp pieces together, measure the length, and add ⁷/₈" for the ring. Measure your wrist and decide how loose or tight you want your bracelet; subtract the clasp/ring measurement. Divide this measurement by two.

2. Cut four 48", one 24", and two 12" floss lengths.

3. The 24" strand is the core strand that the knots are tied around. Thread the needle on the core strand. Slide a bead to the center of the core strand. Place the core strand across the ring with the bead centered in the ring (Fig. 1).

4. Fold two 48" strands in half; attach to one side of the ring with a lark's head knot (page 31), over the core strand (Fig. 2). Repeat for the other side using the 2 remaining 48" lengths.

5. Tape down the strands. Holding 2 strands together as one, tie 2 square knots (page 31) around the core strand on one side of the bracelet (Fig. 3).

6. Slide a bead on the core strand and tie 2 more square knots. Slide another bead on the core strand and tie square knots until the bracelet is the measurement determined in Step 1.

7. Trim the strand ends to 2" and finish the ends (page 32) using the toggle clasp.

8. Repeat Steps 5-7 for the other side of the bracelet.

9. Follow Using Jump Rings (page 32) to attach the charms to the ring.

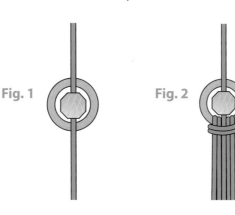

Fig. 1   Fig. 2

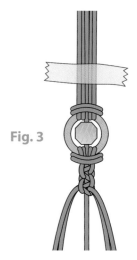

Fig. 3

skinny chevron

To make the Bracelet:

1. Cut two 36" lengths of each color floss. Holding all floss strands together, tie an overhand knot (page 31) about 2" from one end. Tape the knot down.

2. Arrange the floss as shown in **Fig. 1**.

3. Using two strands as a single strand and starting on the left side, make a left knot (page 31) with cream onto orange *(Fig. 2)*. *Remember to tie each knot twice!* Repeat with cream onto gold.

4. Starting on the right side, make a right knot (page 31) with yellow onto brown. *Remember to tie each knot twice!* Repeat with yellow onto cream. A chevron pattern will form *(Fig. 3)*.

5. Go back to the left side and make a left knot with orange on gold and then orange on yellow. On the right side make a right knot with brown on cream and then brown on orange *(Fig. 4)*.

6. Alternating left and right sides, continue knotting in pattern until the bracelet is the length desired. Tie an overhand knot and trim the strands about 2" from the knot.

7. Follow Using Jump Rings (page 32) to attach the charm to the bracelet.

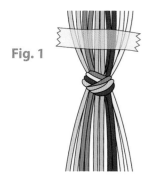

Fig. 1

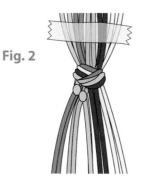

Fig. 2

Fig. 3

Fig. 4

sunset diagonal

To make the Bracelet:

1. Cut two 36" lengths of each color floss. Holding all floss strands together, tie an overhand knot (page 31) about 2" from one end. Tape the knot down.

2. Arrange the floss as shown in Fig. 1.

3. Starting on the left side with rust, make left knots (page 31) across the remaining 9 strands (Fig. 2). *Remember to tie each knot twice!*

Fig. 1

Fig. 2

4. Starting again on the left side with orange, make left knots across the remaining 9 strands *(Fig. 3)*. *Remember to tie each knot twice!*

5. Always starting on the left, repeat Step 3 with light orange, yellow, and light yellow. A diagonal pattern will form *(Fig. 4)*.

6. Leave about 1/2" of unknotted space and then repeat Steps 3-5.

7. Continue knotting and leaving unknotted space until the bracelet is the desired length. Tie an overhand knot and trim the strands about 2" from the knot.

8. Follow Using Jump Rings (page 32) to attach the charm to the bracelet.

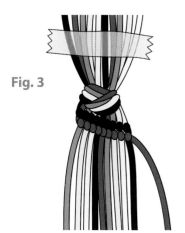

Fig. 3

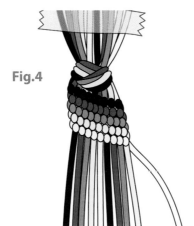

Fig.4

silver butterflies

To make the Bracelet:

1. Cut two 36" light blue and three 36" blue floss lengths. Holding all floss strands together, tie an overhand knot (page 31) about 2" from one end. Tape the knot down *(Fig. 1)*. The center blue strand will always be one of the core strands that the square knots are tied around; the butterfly beads are also placed on this strand. Thread the sewing needle on this center strand.

2. Use the blue strands to tie a square knot around the light blue strands (page 31).

3. Move the blue strands to the center *(Fig. 2)* and tie a square knot around them with the light blue strands *(Fig. 3)*.

4. Repeat Step 3 to move the light blue strands to the center and tie a square knot around them with the blue strands.

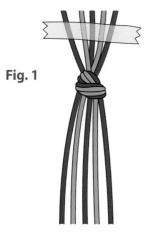

Fig. 1

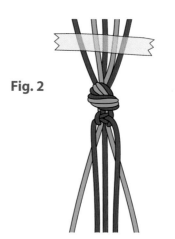

Fig. 2

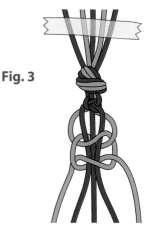

Fig. 3

5. Slide a bead on the center blue strand. Use the blue strands to tie a square knot around the light blue strands under the bead. Referring to **Figs. 2-3**, tie a light blue, then a blue square knot.

6. Slide a bead on the center blue strand. Use the light blue strands to tie a square knot around the blue strands under the bead. Referring to **Figs. 2-3**, tie a blue, then a light blue square knot.

7. Repeat Steps 5-6 until the bracelet is about 1" shorter than the desired finished length. Tie an overhand knot close to the last square knot.

8. Trim the floss ends about $1/4$" from the knot. Place the floss ends in the chain tab ends and add a drop of glue to the floss. Use the pliers to close the tabs in the order shown *(Fig. 4)*.

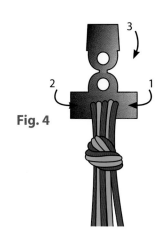

Fig. 4

variegated red sparkle

To make the Bracelet:

1. Cut seven 36" lengths of floss. Holding all floss strands together, tie an overhand knot (page 31) about 2" from one end. Tape the knot down. The middle strand is the core strand that the knots are tied around. Thread the needle on the core strand.

2. Use 3 floss strands together like a single strand. Use the outer strands to make a square knot around the core strand (page 31). Continue making square knots until you have 12 knots. Slide a medium silver bead on the core strand.

3. Make a square knot under the bead (*Fig. 1*). Slide on a small silver bead.

4. Repeat Step 3, sliding on a pink bead, and then the disco ball bead. Reversing the bead order and ending with a square knot, continue adding remaining beads. Make a total of 12 square knots under the last bead. Holding all strands together, tie an overhand knot and trim the strands about 2" from the knot.

Fig. 1

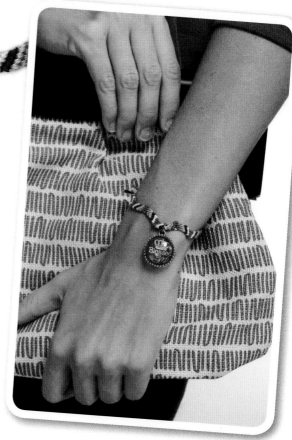

zig-zag

SHOPPING LIST

☐ ecru, brown, light brown, aqua, and green embroidery floss

☐ round metal charm with attached jump ring

☐ 2 pair of chain-nose pliers

To make the Bracelet:

1. Cut two 36" lengths of each color floss. Holding all floss strands together, tie an overhand knot (page 31) about 2" from one end. Tape the ends down.

2. Arrange the floss as shown in **Fig. 1**. *Note: For clarity, Figs. 1-4 show 1 strand only of each color. Knots are tied holding both strands of each color together.*

3. Starting on the left side with ecru, make left knots (page 31) across the remaining 4 strands *(Fig. 2)*. *Remember to tie each knot twice!*

4. Starting again on the left side with brown make left knots across the remaining 4 strands. *Remember to tie each knot twice!*

5. Always starting on the left, repeat Step 3 with aqua, green, and light brown. A diagonal pattern will form *(Fig. 3)*.

6. Remove the tape; turn the bracelet over and tape down again.

7. Start again on the left side with light brown and knot across. Knot in pattern for a total of 6 rows ending with light brown *(Fig. 4)*.

8. Repeat Steps 6-7 until bracelet is the desired length. Holding all strands together, tie an overhand knot and trim the strands about 2" from the knot.

9. Follow Using Jump Rings (page 32) to attach the charm to the bracelet.

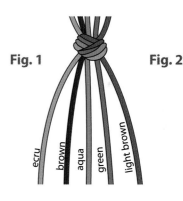

Fig. 1

ecru brown aqua green light brown

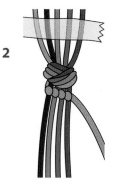

Fig. 2

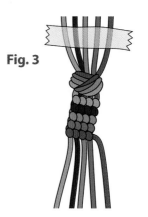

Fig. 3

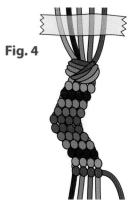

Fig. 4

green satin cord

SHOPPING LIST

- ☐ 4 yards of 2mm green satin cord
- ☐ 2 white/green metal-lined beads
- ☐ 4 green metal-lined beads
- ☐ silver 4-leaf clover bead
- ☐ 2 rhinestone spacer beads
- ☐ 4 silver pony beads

To make the Bracelet:

1. Cut two 72" floss lengths. Holding the strands together, fold the strands in half and tie an overhand knot (page 31) about 1" from fold. Tape the knot down *(Fig. 1)*. The 2 middle strands are the core strands that the knots are tied around.

2. Using the 2 outer strands, tie a square knot (page 31) around the core strands. Continue making square knots until you have 6 knots.

3. Slide a green metal-lined bead on the core strands. Tie a square knot *(Fig. 2)*.

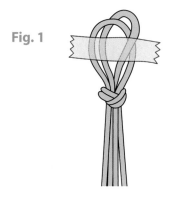

Fig. 1

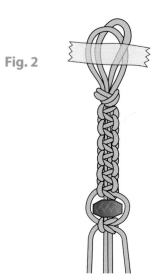

Fig. 2

4. Slide a white/green metal-lined bead on the core strands. Tie a square knot *(Fig. 3)*.

5. Slide a rhinestone bead, a green metal-lined bead, the 4-leaf clover bead, a green metal-lined bead, and a rhinestone bead on the core strands. Tie a square knot *(Fig. 4)*.

6. Repeat Step 4 and then Step 3.

7. Tie 5 more square knots. Holding all 4 cords together, tie an overhand knot. Varying the lengths, trim cord ends to 1¹/₂" -2". Slide a silver bead on each cord; tie an overhand knot under each bead.

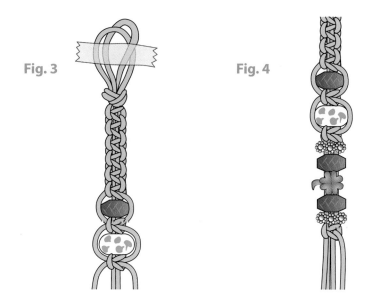

Fig. 3   Fig. 4

DOUBLE-WRAP CRYSTALS

SHOPPING LIST

- ☐ 18mm purple bead
- ☐ 30 6mm lavender faceted beads
- ☐ 60 6mm crystal faceted beads
- ☐ 1½ yards of black braiding cord
- ☐ 1½ yards of silver beading wire

To make the Bracelet:

1. Slide the purple bead to the center of the braiding cord; tie an overhand knot below the bead *(Fig. 1)*.

2. Tie one end of the beading wire around the cords close to the overhand knot; wrap the wire around the cords and trim the wire end *(Fig. 2)*.

3. Refer to Fig. 3 to weave the wire over and under the cords, adding a crystal bead each time the wire crosses between the cords.

4. Continue weaving and adding crystal beads until you have a total of 30 crystal beads. In the same manner, add the 30 lavender beads and then the remaining crystal beads.

5. Holding the cords and the wire together, tie an overhand knot. Tie a knot in the wire only, close to the overhand knot *(Fig. 4)*; trim the wire end. Hide the knot and wire end in the overhand knot.

6. Tie a second overhand knot, about 1" away from the last knot *(Fig. 5)*; trim cord ends.

To wear, wrap the bracelet around your wrist twice and slip the bead through the loop in the cord end.

Fig. 1

Fig. 2

Fig. 3

Fig. 4

Fig. 5

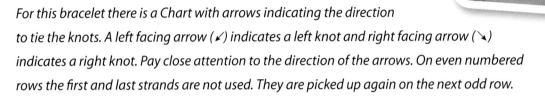

rainbow diagonal

SHOPPING LIST

☐ red, yellow, orange, blue, purple, and white embroidery floss

For this bracelet there is a Chart with arrows indicating the direction to tie the knots. A left facing arrow (↙) indicates a left knot and right facing arrow (↘) indicates a right knot. Pay close attention to the direction of the arrows. On even numbered rows the first and last strands are not used. They are picked up again on the next odd row.

To make the Bracelet:

1. Cut five 36" lengths of white floss and one 36" length of each remaining floss color. Holding all floss strands together, tie an overhand knot (page 31) about 2" from one end. Tape the knot down.

2. Arrange the floss as shown in **Fig. 1**.

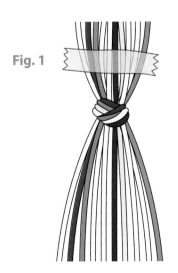

Fig. 1

3. Starting on the left side on Row 1, follow the Knotting Chart to make a left knot (page 31) with white onto red, a right knot (page 31) with white onto orange, a left knot with white onto purple, a right knot with white onto yellow, and a left knot with white onto blue. *Remember to tie each knot twice!*

4. Starting again on the left side on Row 2, follow the Knotting Chart to make a left knot with white onto white, orange onto purple, white onto white, and yellow onto blue. *Remember to tie each knot twice!*

5. Always starting on the left, follow the Knotting Chart for Rows 3-12. Continue knotting in pattern, repeating Rows 1-12, until the bracelet is the length you desire.

6. Tie an overhand knot and trim the strands about 2" from the knot.

Knotting Chart   **Row**

- 1
- 2
- 3
- 4
- 5
- 6
- 7
- 8
- 9
- 10
- 11
- 12

green Beaded Cuff

SHOPPING LIST

- ☐ green embroidery floss
- ☐ 28 square green glass beads
- ☐ 15 round green glass beads
- ☐ 3 sewing needles that will fit through the beads

To make the Bracelet:

1. Cut four 40" lengths and three 15" lengths of floss. Holding the lengths together, tie an overhand knot (page 31) about 2" from one end.

2. Arrange the floss as shown in **Fig. 1**.

3. The knots are tied using groups of 3 floss strands. In a group, the short strand is the core strand the knots are tied around. Using the 3 strands on the left side *(Fig. 2)*, tie 3 square knots (page 31).

4. Using the 3 strands on the right side, tie 3 square knots.

Fig. 1

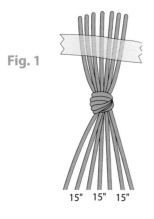

15" 15" 15"

Fig. 2

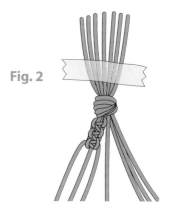

5. Thread the center core strand on a needle and slide a round bead on this strand. Using the 3 strands in the center, tie 3 square knots under the bead *(Fig. 3)*.

6. Thread the core strand of the left group on a needle and slide a square bead on this strand. Using the 3 strands on the left, tie 3 square knots under the bead *(Fig. 4)*.

7. Thread the core strand of the right group on a needle and slide a square bead on this strand. Using the 3 strands on the right, tie 3 square knots under the bead *(Fig. 5)*.

8. Ending with 3 square knots on the outer strands, repeat Steps 5-7 until the bracelet is the right length. Slide a round bead on the center core strand and tie an overhand knot with all strands close to the bead. Trim the strands about 2" from the knot.

Fig. 3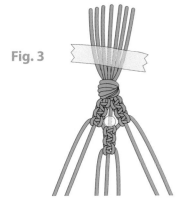

Fig. 4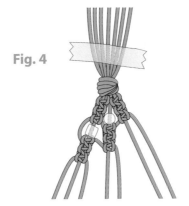

Fig. 5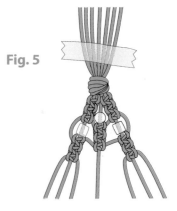

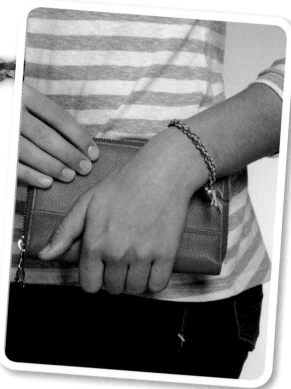

PiNK HaLF-square KNOT SPiRaL

To make the Bracelet:

1. Cut four 36" white, two 36" pink, and two 36" dark pink floss lengths. Holding all floss lengths together, tie an overhand knot (page 31) about 2" from one end. Tape the knot down *(Fig. 1)*. The four white strands are the core strands that the knots are tied around.

2. Use 2 floss strands of the same color together like a single strand. Use the pink and dark pink strands to make the first half of a square knot around the white strands *(Fig. 2)*. Continue making half-square knots until the bracelet is the desired length. As you tie, the knots will spiral around the core strands.

3. Holding all strands together, tie an overhand knot and trim the strands about 2" from the knot.

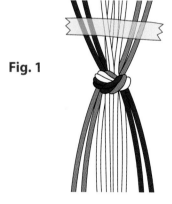

Fig. 1

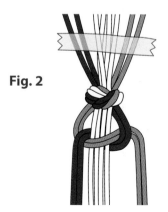

Fig. 2

zig-zag crystals

SHOPPING LIST

- ☐ dark pink embroidery floss
- ☐ 24 medium crystal faceted beads
- ☐ silver toggle clasp
- ☐ silver charm with attached lobster clasp
- ☐ 2 sewing needles that will fit through the beads
- ☐ craft glue

To make the Bracelet:

1. Cut three 36" floss lengths and two 12" lengths. Using one piece of the toggle clasp and one 12" floss length, hold the three 36" lengths together and finish one end (page 32). The middle strand is the core strand that the knots are tied around.

2. Tape down the toggle clasp. Tie a square knot (page 31) around the core strand. Tie another square knot (Fig. 1).

3. Thread a needle on each outer strand.

4. Slide a bead on the right strand. Tie a square knot under the bead (Fig. 2).

5. Slide a bead on the left strand. Tie a square knot under the bead (Fig. 3).

6. Alternating sides, continue adding beads and tying square knots until the bracelet is 1" shorter than the desired finished length.

7. Tie 2 square knots.

8. Finish the end with the remaining toggle clasp piece. Clip the charm on the clasp.

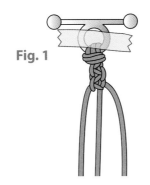

Fig. 1

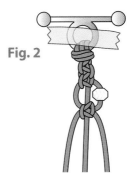

Fig. 2

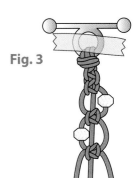

Fig. 3

green print beads

SHOPPING LIST

- ☐ green embroidery floss
- ☐ 3 large green print beads
- ☐ 6 medium green faceted beads
- ☐ sewing needle that will fit through the beads

To make the Bracelet:

1. Cut five 36" floss lengths. Holding all floss lengths together, tie an overhand knot (page 31) about 2" from one end. Tape the knot down *(Fig. 1)*. The middle strand is the core strand that the knots are tied around. Thread the needle on the core strand.

2. Using 2 floss strands held together like a single strand, tie a square knot (page 31) around the core strand. Continue making square knots until you have 8 knots.

3. Slide a faceted bead onto the core strand and tie a square knot *(Fig. 2)*. Add another faceted bead; tie a square knot. Add a green print bead; tie a square knot. Tying 1 square knot between beads, continue adding the remaining beads (1 faceted, 1 green print, 1 faceted, 1 green print, 2 faceted) ; tie 8 square knots.

4. Holding all strands together, tie an overhand knot and trim the strands about 2" from the knot.

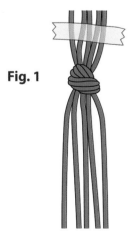

Fig. 1

Fig. 2

Brown center stone

To make the Bracelet:

1. Measure your wrist to see how loose you'd like your bracelet. Add the length of the closed clasp, the length of the cones, and 1¼" for the ring. Subtract this total from your desired bracelet length and divide by two.

2. Slide the beads to the center of the braiding cord. Place the braiding cord across the ring with the beads centered in the ring *(Fig. 1)*.

3. Attach the center of one satin cord length to one side of the ring with a lark's head knot (page 31), over the braiding cord *(Fig. 2)*. Repeat for the other side using the remaining satin cord.

4. Tape down the cords. Make half square knots (page 31) with the satin cord around the braiding cord *(Fig. 3)* until the length is equal to the measurement determined in Step 1.

5. Holding the ends together, tightly wrap a 6" wire length around the cords close to the knots *(Fig. 4)*. Trim the cord ends to 1/2".

6. Thread the wire end through a cone and pull until the cord ends are drawn into the cone *(Fig. 5)*. Trim the wire to 1/2". Make a loop at the wire end (page 32). Use a jump ring (page 32) to attach one end of the toggle clasp.

7. Repeat Steps 4-6 for the other side of the bracelet.

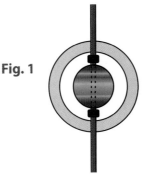

Fig. 1

Fig. 2

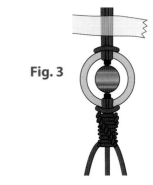

Fig. 3

Fig. 4

Fig. 5

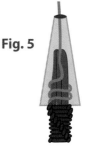

DOUBLE CHEVRON

SHOPPING LIST

☐ ecru, red, yellow, and green embroidery floss

To make the Bracelet:

1. Cut four 36" lengths of each color floss. Holding all the floss strands together, tie an overhand knot (page 31) about 2" from one end. Tape the knot down.

2. Arrange the floss and separate into 4 groups as shown in **Figs. 1-2.**

3. Starting on the left side of Group 1 with yellow, make left knots (page 31) across the remaining 3 strands *(Fig. 3). Remember to tie each knot twice!*

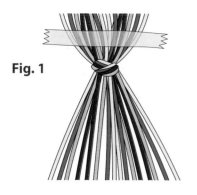

Fig. 1

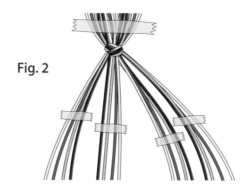

Fig. 2

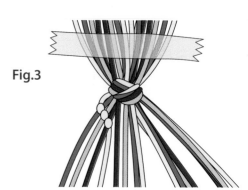

Fig.3

4. Starting on the right side of Group 2 with yellow, make right knots (page 31) across the remaining 3 strands *(Fig. 4)*. *Remember to tie each knot twice!*

5. Make a right knot with the 2 yellow center strands *(Fig. 5)*.

6. Starting on the left side of Group 1 with green, repeat Steps 3-5 *(Fig. 6)*.

7. Repeat Steps 3-6 with Group 3 and Group 4. *(Fig. 7)*

8. At this point there is a left V and a right V. To connect the V's, tie a right knot with the 2 ecru center strands (1 from Group 2 and 1 from Group 3) as shown in Fig 8.

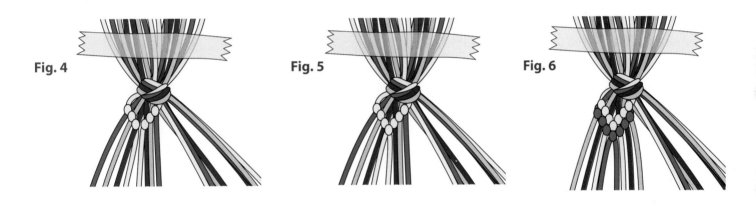

Fig. 4   Fig. 5   Fig. 6

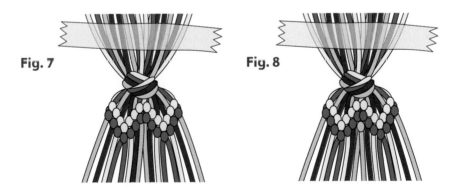

Fig. 7   Fig. 8

Continued on page 24.

Double Chevron continued.

9. Starting on the left side of Group 1 with ecru, make left knots across the remaining 3 strands. Starting on the right side of Group 2 with ecru, make right knots across the remaining 3 strands. Make a right knot with the 2 ecru center strands. Repeat for Groups 3-4 *(Fig. 9)*.

10. Repeat Step 8 to join the 2 red center strands and Step 9 to tie the red row *(Fig. 10)*.

11. Continue in pattern, repeating Steps 8-9 until bracelet is the desired length. Holding all strands together, tie an overhand knot and trim the strands about 2" from knot.

Fig. 9

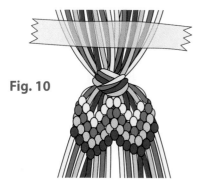

Fig. 10

peacock Feather

To make the Bracelet:

1. Cut two 54" lengths of each color floss. Holding all floss strands together, tie an overhand knot (page 31) about 2" from one end. Tape the knot down.

2. Arrange the floss as shown in **Fig. 1**.

3. Starting on the left side and working toward the middle, make left knots (page 31) with black across 3 strands *(Fig. 2)*. *Remember to tie each knot twice!*

4. Starting on the right side and working toward the middle, make right knots (page 31) with black across 3 strands *(Fig. 3)*. *Remember to tie each knot twice!*

5. Make a right knot with black on black in the center forming the chevron "V" *(Fig. 4)*.

6. Start again on the left side and make left knots with teal across 3 strands. Make right knots with teal across 3 strands and a teal right knot in the center *(Fig. 5)*.

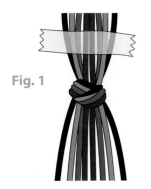

Fig. 1

Fig. 2

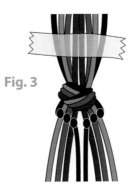

Fig. 3

Fig. 4

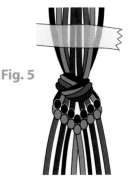

Fig. 5

Continued on page 26.

Peacock Feather continued.

7. Repeat Step 6 with blue and then with purple.

8. On the left side, make a left knot and then a right knot with black onto teal. On the right side, make a right knot and then a left knot with black onto teal *(Fig. 6)*.

9. Starting in the center with the left purple strand and working toward the left, make right knots across the next 3 strands. Starting with the right purple strand and working toward the right, make left knots across the next 3 strands, forming a purple "X" *(Fig. 7)*.

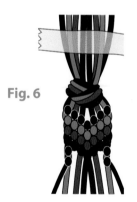

Fig. 6

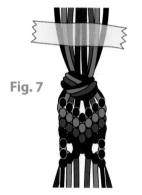

Fig. 7

10. Make a right knot with blue on blue in the center. With the left blue strand, make right knots across the next 2 strands. With the right blue strand, make left knots across the next 2 strands. Repeat with teal to make center knot and to make left and right knots onto the black strands. Make a right knot with black onto black in the center *(Fig. 8)*.

11. Make a left knot with the left teal strand onto the left black strand. Make a right knot with the right teal strand onto the right black strand. Make a center knot with teal on teal *(Fig. 9)*.

12. Repeat Step 11 with blue across 2 strands and with purple across 3 strands *(Fig. 10)*.

13. Repeat Steps 8-12 until the bracelet is 1" shorter than the desired length.

14. Work Steps 3-7 in reverse order to complete the bracelet. Tie an overhand knot and trim the strands about 2" from the knot.

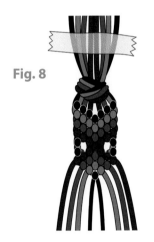

Fig. 8

Fig. 9

Fig. 10

sparkling diamonds

SHOPPING LIST

☐ white, orange, yellow, and grey embroidery floss

To make the Bracelet:

1. Cut two 36" lengths of each color floss. Holding all floss strands together, tie an overhand knot (page 31) about 2" from one end. Tape the knot down.

2. Arrange the floss as shown in **Fig. 1**.

3. Starting in the center, make a left knot (page 31) with the 2 white center strands *(Fig. 2)*. *Remember to tie each knot twice!*

4. With the center right white strand make left knots onto the grey, yellow, and orange strands *(Fig. 3)*. *Remember to tie each knot twice!*

5. With the center left white strand make right knots (page 31) onto the grey, yellow and orange strands *(Fig. 4)*. *Remember to tie each knot twice!*

6. Repeat Steps 3-5 with grey, yellow, and then orange *(Fig. 5)*.

7. Make a left knot with the 2 center white strands *(Fig. 6)*.

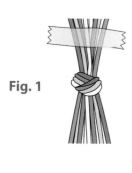

Fig. 1

Fig. 2

Fig. 3

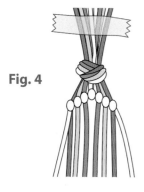

Fig. 4

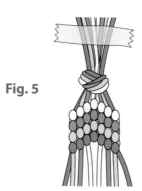

Fig. 5

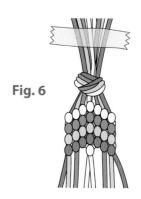

Fig. 6

8. Make a right knot with the right center white strand onto the grey strand *(Fig. 7)*. *You will be crossing over the grey to tie with the white.*

9. Make a left knot with the left center white strand onto the grey strand *(Fig. 8)*. *You will be crossing over the grey to tie with the white.*

10. Make a left knot with the 2 center white strands *(Fig. 9)*.

11. On the left side, make left knots with orange onto yellow, grey, and white. On the right side, make right knots with orange onto yellow, grey, and white. Make a left knot with the 2 center orange strands *(Fig. 10)*.

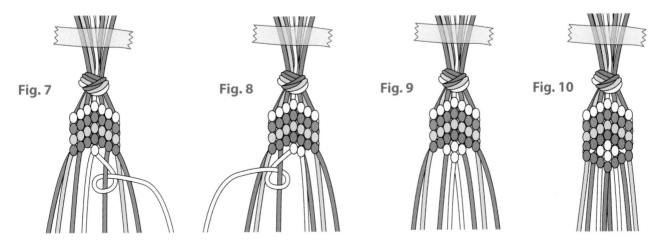

Fig. 7   **Fig. 8**   **Fig. 9**   **Fig. 10**

Continued on page 30.

12. Repeat Step 11 with yellow *(Fig. 11)*.

13. On the left side, make left knots with grey onto white then orange. On the right side, make right knots with grey onto white then orange *(Fig. 12)*.

14. On the left side, make a right knot with white onto orange. On the right side, make a left knot with white onto orange *(Fig. 13)*. **You will be crossing over the grey to tie with the white.**

15. Make a right knot with the left grey onto orange and then white. Make a left knot with the right grey onto orange and then white *(Fig. 14)*.

16. Make a left knot with the 2 center yellow strands. Make left knots with the yellow left center strand onto orange, white, and grey. Make right knots with the yellow right center strand onto orange, white, and grey *(Fig. 15)*.

17. Starting back in the center with orange, repeat Step 16 across the white, grey, and yellow strands *(Fig. 16)*.

18. Repeat Steps 7-17 until your bracelet is the desired length (for a 6³/₄" bracelet, we made 7 diamond repeats and stopped after a Step 12). Tie an overhand knot and trim the floss about 2" from the knot.

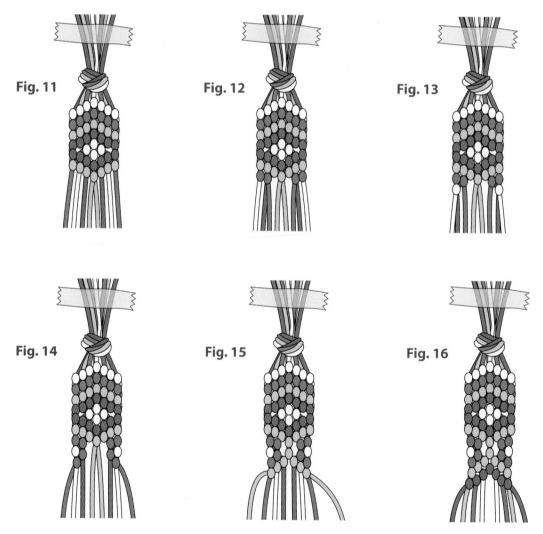

Fig. 11   Fig. 12   Fig. 13

Fig. 14   Fig. 15   Fig. 16

general instructions

KNOTS

Overhand Knot (loose or folded ends)

Hold the strands together and tie a knot *(Figs. 1-2)*.

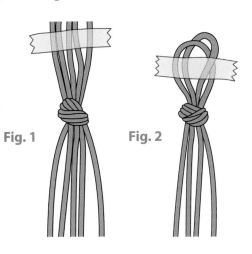

Fig. 1   Fig. 2

Lark's Head Knot

Slip the loop through the metal ring. Pull the ends through the loop and tighten *(Fig. 3)*.

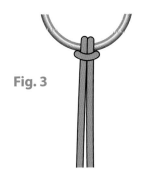

Fig. 3

Square Knot

Use the outer strand(s) to tie the first half of a square knot *(Fig. 4)*.

Use the outer strand(s) to tie the second half of a square knot *(Fig. 5)*.

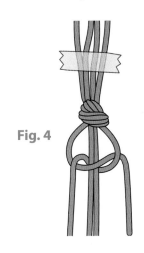

Fig. 4

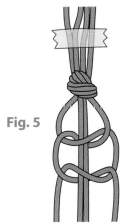

Fig. 5

Half-Square Knot

Refer to Fig. 4 to tie the first half only of a square knot; repeat until you reach the desired length. As you tie, the knots will spiral.

Left Knot

Begin with the strands on the left side. Wrap around the center strands and pull upward to tighten. To complete each left knot, always tie again, using the same strands *(Fig. 6-7)*.

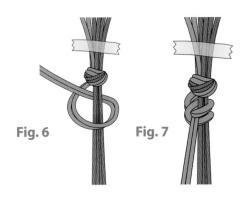

Fig. 6   Fig. 7

Right Knot

Begin with the strands on the right side. Wrap around the center strands and pull upward to tighten. To complete each right knot, always tie again, using the same strands *(Fig. 8-9)*.

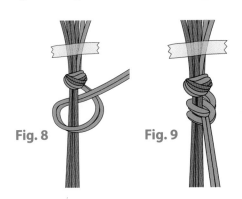

Fig. 8   Fig. 9

FINISHING

Using Jump Rings

Pick up a jump ring with a pair of chain-nose pliers. With a second pair of chain-nose pliers, gently hold the other side of the ring. Open the ring by pulling one pair of pliers toward you while pushing the other away *(Fig. 10)*.

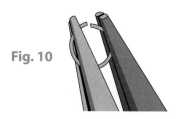

Fig. 10

Close the ring by pushing and pulling the pliers in opposite directions, bringing the ring ends back together. Open and close chain links and loops on eye pins or head pins the same way.

Making a Bead Dangle, Connector or Loops on Wire

Bead Dangles are made on head pins and have a loop at one end. Connectors are made on eye pins and have loops on both ends. Loops on wire ends are made in the same manner as the loops on bead dangles and connectors.

Slide the beads on a head pin or eye pin. Leaving about ¹/₂", cut off the excess wire. Using chain-nose pliers, bend the wire at a 90° angle *(Fig. 11)*. Grasp the wire end with the round-nose pliers. Turn the pliers and bend the wire into a loop *(Fig. 12)*. Release the pliers. Straighten or twist the loop further if necessary.

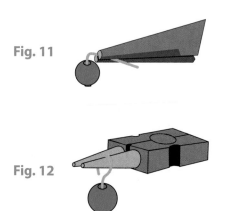

Fig. 11

Fig. 12

Finishing Ends

Holding the strands together and leaving 1" tails, fold the floss over a jump ring or clasp *(Fig. 13)*.

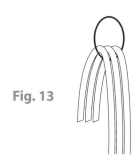

Fig. 13

Form a loop with one 12" length of floss. Wrap the length around the folded strands 4-5 times. Bring the end through the loop. Pull firmly on the opposite end of the cord until the loop disappears *(Fig. 14)*.

Place a drop of glue on the knot. When the glue is dry, trim the ends *(Fig. 15)*.

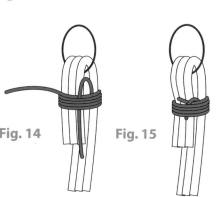

Fig. 14   Fig. 15

Production Team: Craft Design Director – Patti Wallenfang; Designer – Kelly Reider; Technical Writer – Jean Lewis; Technical Associate – Mary Sullivan Hutcheson; Editorial Writer – Susan Frantz Wiles; Senior Graphic Artist – Lora Puls; Graphic Artist – Cailen Cochran; Photostylist – Lori Wenger; Photographer –Jason Masters.